Understanding
and Managing Stress:

A Facilitator's Guide

Understanding and Managing Stress:

A Facilitator's Guide

John D. Adams

University Associates, Inc.
8517 Production Avenue
P.O. Box 26240
San Diego, CA 92126

PREFACE

The material in this manual is a fairly detailed description of the approach to stress and stress-management training that I have developed over the past several years. A typical, two-day training design is presented, along with suggestions for the facilitator conducting a workshop using the materials presented in *Understanding and Managing Stress: A Workbook in Changing Life Styles.* Thus, it is assumed that the facilitator has a copy of this workbook and is familiar with its contents. An additional source of information is *Understanding and Managing Stress: A Book of Readings.*

Each facilitator certainly will have his own ideas about teaching people to live with stress successfully. This manual simply provides a starting point for such instruction and, hopefully, some new ideas to supplement those of the facilitator.

The first chapter presents the prework activity concept, an overview of the sample training design, and a statement of the objectives used in my own workshops. Chapter 2 deals with the facilitator's role; it is based on my viewpoint that stress management is a unique and complex topic and on my recommendation that the facilitator possess a high level of content knowledge as well as group-training skills. Chapter 3 covers prework, or the work to be completed by the facilitator and the participants in advance of the workshop. Chapters 4 through 7 present the sequence of the typical workshop design, with each chapter covering approximately half of a day of training.

I am aware that many women are involved in stress-management training. However, in order to avoid the cumbersome use of "he/she" and to conform to the publisher's editorial policies, I have used the designation "he" throughout.

Just as my own approach to stress management is constantly changing, I am sure that each facilitator will develop unique and innovative training techniques. I am extremely interested in learning of any suggestions arising from the use of these materials.

April, 1980   John D. Adams, Ph.D.
                                                               Arlington, Virginia

CONTENTS

CHAPTER 1

INTRODUCTION OF TWO-DAY DESIGN

WORKSHOP STRUCTURE

The stress-workshop design consists of five important elements:

1. Prework;
2. Overview of the stress response and personal diagnosis;
3. Self-management techniques;
4. Creation and use of support networks;
5. Organizational improvement and personal action planning.

Although any number of people conceivably could participate in the workshop, the author has found that a group of twenty-four is ideal and that a group of fewer than twelve does not present the advantage of a sufficient variety of viewpoints.

Prework

In addition to planning several aspects of the workshop in advance, the facilitator should consider the advantages of having the participants complete several of the training activities prior to arriving at the workshop. This practice saves time, generates a data base, and starts the participants thinking about their present stress levels and responses to stress. The process of completing and scoring these specific activities takes about an hour.

Overview and Diagnosis

The overview and diagnosis segment of the workshop (covered in Module I of the workbook) reviews the physiology and psychology of stress and presents a summarized form of some of the prework data with which the participants can compare their scores. This segment takes approximately three and a half hours.

Self-Management

The self-management segment (Modules II and III) covers nutrition, exercise, self-awareness, letting-go techniques (meditation and so on), and personal planning (time management and life/career planning[1]). The participants assess their present self-management habits and learn a great deal about each of these subjects. This segment requires a minimum of four and a half hours.

Support Networks

The support-network segment (Module IV) provides the participants with an opportunity to assess their present sources of support and the quality of that support. It also provides a format for planning the improvement of support networks. This segment can be completed in approximately two hours.

Organizational Improvement and Personal Action Planning

The first part of this segment covers organizational improvement (Module V). The participants assess their levels of work-related stress, reviewing the data from the applicable prework activities. They then develop plans for changing their organizations in accordance with the goal of removing unnecessary stressors.

Finally, the participants are given time to review the workshop information and activities presented and are asked to develop personal action plans for improved stress management (Module VI). The entire segment, including both organizational improvement and personal action planning, takes approximately four hours.

OBJECTIVES

The objectives most commonly presented to participants in the workshop are as follows:

---

[1]The workbook covers both time management and life/career planning. However, the proposed workshop structure does not include sufficient time for dealing with both considerations. Chapter 5 of this manual offers a workshop presentation of both subjects so that the facilitator can choose the one that best meets the needs of the participants. If the facilitator wants to cover both subjects, the two-day workshop design must be altered accordingly.

- To explain what stress is, where it comes from, and what it can do to people;
- To diagnose the participants' present sources and levels of stress;
- To enable the participants to analyze their individual responses to stress;
- To guide the participants in developing personal plans of action for improved stress management after reviewing a variety of proven techniques.

The facilitator should emphasize to the participants that fostering expertise in stress management is not one of the objectives of the workshop; entire careers easily could be spent investigating any one of the specific topics presented. Instead, the main goal is to create an awareness of and interest in stress so that the participants decide to pursue the subject further on their own after the workshop.

DESIGN OUTLINE

If possible, this two-day design should cover at least the period from 8:30 a.m. to 4:30 p.m. each day. This amount of time is the minimum required to cover all of the aspects of stress and stress management presented in the following outline. An evening session or additional time each afternoon allows further exploration of individual topics; adding additional aspects without excluding any of those listed below requires a third day of training. This outline is explained in detail in subsequent chapters of this manual.

DAY 1

Time	Presentation	Duration
8:30 a.m.	1. Opening session 　a. Breathing exercise 　b. Overview design 　c. Objectives and assumptions 　d. Selection of partners	Thirty minutes
9:00	2. Physiology and psychology of stress 　a. Slides and/or lecture 　b. Discussion	One hour
10:00	BREAK	Fifteen minutes

DAY 1 (cont.)

Time	Presentation	Duration
10:15	3. Stress-management review a. Activity completion b. Small-group sharing c. Inventory of techniques	One hour
11:15	4. Prework stress evaluations a. Feedback b. Discussion	Forty-five minutes
12:00 Noon	LUNCH	One hour
1:00 p.m.	5. Comparison of life-style habits a. Activity completion b. Lecture c. Discussion	Thirty minutes
1:30	6. Prework nutrition and exercise evaluations a. Feedback b. Discussion	Fifteen minutes
1:45	BREAK	Fifteen minutes
2:00	7. Consideration of time management *or* life/career planning	Two hours
4:00	8. Progressive relaxation and meditation experience	Thirty minutes

DAY 2

Time	Presentation	Duration
8:30 a.m.	9. Life-style preferences a. Activity completion b. Group discussion c. Lecture	One hour
9:30	10. Lecture/discussion on support networks	Fifteen minutes
9:45	BREAK	Fifteen minutes
10:00	11. Completion of Support-Network Review	Thirty minutes

DAY 2 (cont.)

Time	Presentation	Duration
10:30	12. Support-network improvement a. Activity completion b. Work with partners	One hour
11:30	13. Organizational-stress data a. Review of prework scores on work-related stress evaluations b. Discussion of most pervasive stressors and coping with them	Thirty minutes
12:00 Noon	LUNCH	One hour
1:00 p.m.	14. Job suitability a. Activity completion b. Lecture/discussion	Thirty minutes
1:30	15. Organizational-improvement proposals a. Small-group work b. Discussion	One hour
2:30	BREAK	Fifteen minutes
2:45	16. Personal planning a. Activity completion b. Work with partners	One hour
3:45	17. Completion of Workshop Evaluation	Fifteen minutes
4:00	18. Relaxation, meditation, or self-healing experience	Thirty minutes

CHAPTER 2

THE FACILITATOR'S ROLE

To help ensure a successful workshop, the facilitator should be obviously serious about his own life style and approach to managing stress. He should demonstrate that he has control of his life and that he has made a personal investment in stress management. For example, the facilitator who is overweight and smokes should be aware that the credibility of the workshop might suffer as a result; also, the facilitator who is poorly educated about stress and its management should expect problems. This chapter deals with the knowledge and skills the author recommends that the facilitator possess.

KNOWLEDGE

The facilitator's knowledge about stress and its management is of great importance in the workshop. Interest in stress has escalated greatly; as a result, a tremendous variety of stress-management approaches and techniques has been developed. Further, many of the specific disciplines in the area of stress management, particularly nutrition and exercise, are subjects of great controversy among their respective proponents. It is important to become familiar with these controversies and adopt a personal opinion because many different viewpoints are likely to be represented in the workshop group.

Participating in stress-management seminars, courses, and workshops is one good way to develop this knowledge. Also, reading books such as the following can be extremely helpful:

SUBJECT	AUTHOR	TITLE
Overview of stress management	McCamy and Presley	*Human Life Styling: Keeping Whole in the Twentieth Century*

7

SUBJECT	AUTHOR	TITLE
Physiology and psychology of stress	McQuade and Aikman	*Stress*
Nutrition	Williams	*Nutrition Against Disease*
Exercise	Cooper	*The New Aerobics*
Letting go	Pelletier	*Mind as Healer Mind as Slayer*
Self-awareness	Rogers	*On Personal Power*
Time management	Webber	*Time and Management*
Life/career planning	Kirn and Kirn	*Life Work Planning*
Support networks	Kirschenbaum and Glaser	*Developing Support Groups*
Stress in organizations	Kahn, et al.	*Organizational Stress: Studies in Role Conflict and Ambiguity*

Refer to the list of *SUGGESTED READINGS* at the end of each module in the workbook for more complete references.

SKILLS

The facilitator not only must possess conceptual skills to assimilate and interpret information about stress management; he also must possess experiential-training skills to be able to create meaningful learning experiences for the participants and to keep the workshop from becoming simply a conceptual seminar.

In addition, the facilitator who is a competent organizational consultant has a distinct advantage. The two major emphases of the workshop are individual life-style change and organizational change. The focus on organizational change is difficult to maintain in many workshops because of the enormous interest in the life-style change considerations. In order to maintain a balance between the two emphases, the facilitator must provide a natural transition from the subject of individual stress management to the consideration of eliminating unnecessary stress in organizations.

Flexibility is another important characteristic of the successful facilitator. Some groups want to concentrate on nutrition while others prefer devoting extra time to changing stressor norms at work. The facilitator must be able to alter the workshop design to meet the group's needs; he may find it necessary to create activities at a moment's notice, accelerate or decelerate the process, and so on. Each group is unique, and it is seldom possible to complete the entire design with which the workshop starts.

Finally, the facilitator is the center of attention throughout the workshop. The energy, interest, and involvement he manifests are highly visible to the participants, whose own energy and interest will rise and fall. Therefore, the facilitator must be able to constantly convey enthusiasm and keep the participants involved when their energy and interest are waning.

CHAPTER 3

PREWORK

A certain amount of prework, or work completed in advance of the workshop, is advisable for the participants as well as the facilitator. The facilitator should be aware of the possibility and convenience of having the participants complete some of the workbook activities prior to arriving at the workshop. In fact, some facilitators might want participants to complete all of the activities and read the entire workbook before attending the workshop.

PARTICIPANTS' PREWORK

The suggested practice is to send out the workbook, along with a cover letter welcoming the participants and asking them to read the Introduction and complete the prework activities[2] in advance of the workshop. The facilitator also encloses a summary sheet on which to record the prework activity scores. The letter requests that the summary sheets be returned to the facilitator about ten days before the workshop so that the facilitator can rank the participants' scores and become familiar with the intensity and sources of stress within the group. In the cover letter, the facilitator reminds the participants to bring their workbooks and completed prework activities with them to the workshop. The activities designated for prework are the following:

ACTIVITY	PAGE IN WORKBOOK
Episodic, Work-Related Stress Evaluation	15
Episodic, Nonwork-Related Stress Evaluation	17

[2]The prework activities are listed separately in the workbook table of contents.

ACTIVITY	PAGE IN WORKBOOK
Chronic, Work-Related Stress Evaluation	19
Chronic, Nonwork-Related Stress Evaluation	21
Life and Career Assessment[3]	40
Nutrition Evaluation	48
Physical-Exercise Evaluation	52

The participants may compare their scores on all of these activities except the Life and Career Assessment with the percentile scores included in the workbook text.

FACILITATOR'S PREWORK

The facilitator must determine the types of food available for breaks and meals and inform the food-services manager about these needs. The author suggests that the sponsoring organization provide juices, herbal teas, and fresh fruit as alternatives to coffee and doughnuts at break time. He further suggests that meals be low in sugar, salt, saturated fat (red meat and so on), white flour, and chemical additives. However, if caffeine and doughnuts are completely unavailable or if a totally vegetarian meal is served, the facilitator can expect some complaints about lack of free choice. Also, heavy coffee drinkers may develop headaches late in the day due to caffeine withdrawal. Given a choice, though, most workshop participants opt for the healthful alternative.

Audiovisual needs are another concern of the facilitator. These needs should be clearly communicated to the sponsoring organization. The author generally uses a carrousel slide projector and a cassette synchronizer for the slide-tape overview presentation on the first morning, a 16-millimeter projector for a time-management film on the first afternoon, and a cassette recorder to play music during breaks and relaxation periods.

---

[3]The Life and Career Assessment is used as prework only if the facilitator's workshop design includes the life/career-planning segment of Module II; it is not used if the facilitator opts for time management instead of life/career planning. As an alternative, it can be assigned as overnight homework after the first day of the workshop if the life/career-planning segment is scheduled for the second day.

CHAPTER 4

OPENING SESSION

The purpose of the opening session is to cover the first two objectives of the workshop, to help the participants understand the stress-response process and to aid them in diagnosing their present levels of stress.

OVERVIEW

The first workshop experience should be a meaningful one. A good way to begin is to ask participants to sit comfortably with their eyes closed and concentrate on their breathing for a few minutes. During this period, play some relaxing music.

After the experience, discuss the following purposes for it:

- It helps to relax people and may even lower their blood pressures for a few minutes.
- Under stress, people tend to breathe very shallowly or hold their breaths. This activity provides a practical suggestion to do some deep breathing when entering a stressful situation.
- The workshop participants, like most people, probably tend to dwell on the unfinished business in their lives. The breathing exercise helps the participants forget about such unfinished business for the present and focus on the situation at hand, the workshop.

After the breathing experience and a presentation of its purposes, briefly review the workshop design, objectives, and training assumptions. (At this point the author also adds his assumptions that the participants are attending voluntarily and that each will manage his or her own level of self-disclosure.)

Ask the participants to introduce themselves. Request that they stand up and walk around the room, each eventually selecting a partner with whom to work. Emphasize that the choice of a partner should be a thoughtful one because some of the workshop activities can become frustrating if the partners are incompatible. Encourage the participants to select partners with whom they feel they can talk and explore situations easily and who have similar levels of motivation regarding the workshop.

When partners have been selected, it is a good idea to show a twenty-minute slide presentation called "Understanding Stress," which is available from Greater Southeast Community Hospital, 1310 Southern Avenue, S.E., Washington, D.C. 20032. Follow the slides with a lecture and/or discussion of the stress process, using Figure 7 in the workbook (p. 24) as a focal point and incorporating the Coronary-Risk Profile (workbook, p. 31).

Then ask the participants to complete the Stress-Management Review Form and the following unfinished statements (workbook, p. 25).

STRESS-MANAGEMENT REVIEW

Goals   To increase the participants' awareness of their present responses to stress, both effective and ineffective.

To provide preliminary ideas for improved stress management.

To develop a total-group inventory of effective responses to stress.

Format   Individual, small-group, and total-group work.

Duration   One hour.

Materials   Stress-Management Review Form and the following unfinished statements (workbook, p. 25), pencils, newsprint flip charts, felt-tipped markers, and tape or hardware for hanging newsprint on the wall.

Setting   Room with writing surfaces for the participants and large enough to allow the entire group to meet in small subgroups.

Process   1. Allow the participants twenty minutes to complete the form and the unfinished statements.

2. Ask the participants to form small groups of four to six, partners remaining together, and spend fifteen minutes sharing responses to the first unfinished statement. Have each group appoint one member to serve as a recorder of responses.

3. As the recorders report the groups' ideas, record them on newsprint. Hang each sheet on the wall when it is filled, creating an inventory of group members' presently used effective responses to stress.

4. Spend fifteen minutes leading a discussion on the overall list.

Remarks

1. Emphasize at the outset that the participants will be asked to share only their most effective responses to stress; the rest of what they write down is for their own private use.

2. The overall inventory accomplishes the following:
   - Because it will include many proven stress-management techniques, it reinforces much of the workshop content.
   - Everyone present derives a sense of the participants' range of experience, which helps in determining the level at which to present the remainder of the workshop.
   - Most of the effective responses will be of the immediate type (see Figure 1). Since the major focus of the workshop will be on two other types of responses, stress avoidance and long-term protection, it is important that these effective immediate responses to stress receive attention here.

3. Invite reactions to the overall inventory. As a part of the developing discussion, introduce Figure 1 both as a way of describing the nature of the inventory and as the framework for an integrated strategy for stress management that sets the stage for the remainder of the workshop. The idea of an integrated strategy for stress management is that an organization and its members, in order to cope successfully with stress, must respond effectively in each of the six areas represented by the boxes in Figure 1.

STRESS-MANAGEMENT RESPONSES

		Individual	Organization
TYPE OF RESPONSE	Removal or Avoidance	• Self-awareness • Personal planning (time management and life/career planning) • Supportive relationships	• Complete, two-way information flow • Identification and change of stressor norms • Decision making and policy formulation • Reassignments
	Immediate Response	• Conflict skills • Influencing skills • Assertive skills • Problem-solving skills • Change in expectations • Supportive relationships	• Problem identification • Diagnosis • Problem solving • Employee education • Employee-assistance programs
	Long-Term Protection	• Effective self-management (nutrition, exercise, and relaxation) • Supportive relationships	• Active support and encouragement of good self-management practices on the part of organization members • Informal support groups

Figure 1. Integrated Strategy for Stress Management

The last activity of the first half-day is the feedback and discussion of the rank-ordered prework scores for the four stressor evaluations in the workbook (Episodic, Work-Related Stress Evaluation, p. 15; Episodic, Nonwork-Related Stress Evaluation, p. 17; Chronic, Work-Related Stress Evaluation, p. 19; and Chronic, Nonwork-Related Stress Evaluation, p. 21). Encourage the participants to identify the locations of their own scores within the respective rank-ordered lists and to compare their scores with the percentile scores provided in Table 3 (workbook, p. 23) to see how they and their group compare with a larger population.

Participants' selections of the top three stressors from the Episodic, Work-Related Stress Evaluation and the Chronic, Work-Related Stress Evaluation are not fed back at this time but are saved for a discussion that opens the organizational-improvement segment of the workshop.

CHAPTER 5

SECOND SESSION

The second half-day focuses on the ways in which the participants can avoid some of the stress in their lives and improve their physical, psychological, and spiritual fitness for withstanding stress in the long run.

The elements to be covered in this half-day of the sample design are as follows:

- Comparison of life-style habits (focus on nutrition and exercise);
- Time management *or* life/career planning (facilitator chooses);
- Relaxation and meditation.

COMPARISON OF LIFE-STYLE HABITS

Goals   To provide an opportunity for the participants to assess their present life-style habits.

To mobilize the participants' concerns about the ways in which they presently take care of themselves.

Format   Individual and total-group work.

Duration   Forty-five minutes.

Materials   Appraisal of Life-Style Habits (workbook, p. 8), pencils, newsprint flip charts, and felt-tipped markers.

Setting   Room large enough for the total group and with writing surfaces for the participants.

Process   1. Ask the participants to complete the Appraisal of Life-Style Habits. Discuss each habit.

2. Present the health and mortality data in Table 2 (workbook, p. 9).

3. Feed back and discuss the rank-ordered scores on the prework Nutrition Evaluation (workbook, p. 48) and Physical-Exercise Evaluation (workbook, p. 52).

Remarks

1. Discussing the Appraisal of Life-Style Habits offers the opportunity to present additional materials or activities on each of the habits dealt with in the appraisal, if desired, thus extending the time required.

2. When feeding back the Nutrition Evaluation and Physical-Exercise Evaluation scores, encourage the participants to compare their scores with those of the other participants and with the percentile scores presented in Table 7 (workbook, p. 50) and Table 8 (workbook, p. 53).

3. One caution is in order. As mentioned before, the various schools of thought concerning nutrition and exercise present many contradictions, controversies, and logical but mutually exclusive approaches. If any one approach is advocated, the chances are good that at least one participant will strongly disagree and cite evidence to negate the chosen approach.

The author, who has concluded that each of the approaches is right for some people, explains his personal approaches to workshop participants and encourages them to educate themselves and discover the alternatives that work best for them. The important point is that the workshop design is too full to spend a great deal of time debating with the participants.

TIME MANAGEMENT[4]

Goals

To provide an understanding of the basic principles of good time management.

To analyze the participants' main sources of wasted time.

---

[4]In the proposed workshop design, the facilitator presents either this segment or the life/career-planning segment that follows. If the facilitator chooses to cover both segments, the two-day workshop design must be altered accordingly.

To ensure that the participants begin to plan for more effective time usage.

Format   Total-group work, individual work, and work with partners.

Duration   Two hours.

Materials   Time-management film, screen, 16-millimeter projector, Sources of Wasted Time at Work (workbook, p. 36), Job-Time Analysis Form (workbook, p. 38), and pencils.

Setting   Room with writing surfaces for the participants and large enough to allow partners to work together without intrusion from other pairs.

Process   1. Show a time-management film such as "The Time of Your Life" or "A Perfectly Normal Day." (Both films may be rented from the Cally-Curtis Company, 1111 N. Las Palmas Avenue, Hollywood, California 90038.)

2. Lecture and/or lead a discussion on time-management principles, using the workbook material to summarize the basic principles and techniques of good time management.

3. Ask the participants to complete the list of Sources of Wasted Time at Work.

4. Compare the participants' lists with the list of the top fifteen time wasters on p. 37 of the workbook. Discuss ways to deal with these time wasters.

5. Ask the participants to complete the Job-Time Analysis Form.

6. Have the partners consult each other regarding their job-time analyses. Use the five questions listed on p. 39 of the workbook as a starting point.

7. Spend some time sharing experiences in the total group.

Remarks   1. The two suggested films summarize the work of time-management expert Lakein. "The Time of Your Life" describes six principles for managing discretionary time, which is the time that is under a person's control. "A Perfectly Normal Day" investigates problems associated with interruptions and other types of nondiscretionary time.

2. The author prefers the work of Webber (1972) for providing an overview of time-management principles and techniques. The core of his approach is included in the workbook (p. 37).

3. Prepare to discuss the major time wasters and their removal by becoming familiar with Mackenzie's book, *The Time Trap* (1972).

4. In presenting the Job-Time Analysis Form, suggest that the participants try to break down their jobs into specific tasks, which will give them a better possibility of finding areas for change.

5. The total-group sharing at the end need not be long, but it is important in that it provides closure to the activities and an indication of whether they were valuable to the participants.

6. As part of the total-group sharing, point out that the Job-Time Analysis Form is subjective. Encourage the participants to keep actual time logs of their activities for a week or two, and suggest that they will be surprised at the results. Also, ask them to consider having a consultant observe their time usage for a day.

LIFE/CAREER PLANNING[5]

Goals   To have the participants review and describe their life and/or career situations.

To start the participants exploring the aspects of their life and/or career situations over which they have control.

To ensure that the participants begin to make plans for exercising more personal control over their life and/or career situations.

---

[5]In the proposed workshop design, the facilitator presents either this segment or the preceding time-management segment. If the facilitator chooses to cover both segments, the two-day workshop design must be altered accordingly.

Format   Prework activity, work with partners, and total-group work.

Duration   Two hours.

Materials   Life and Career Assessment (workbook, p. 40), Self-Analysis and Guide for Life and Career Planning (workbook, p. 43), and pencils.

Setting   Room with writing surfaces for the participants and large enough to allow partners to work together without intrusion from other pairs.

Process   1. Ask the partners to spend fifteen minutes sharing their prework responses to the Life and Career Assessment.

2. Ask partner A to interview partner B for thirty-five to forty minutes, spending about five minutes per question probing for additional insights. Ask partner A to write partner B's responses in partner B's book.

3. Have the participants switch roles and repeat the interview process.

4. Spend a few minutes sharing experiences in the total group.

Remarks   1. Sharing the prework responses to the Life and Career Assessment assists the partners in developing rapport and establishing clear pictures of their present life and/or career situations.

2. The interview format allows the interviewee to think things through and be creative without having to write down these thoughts. The interviewer should not only record the partner's comments but also assist the partner's explorations by means of good coaching and interviewing techniques such as the following:

   • Asking open-ended questions and otherwise encouraging the partner to talk;

   • Expressing warmth and interest;

   • Actively listening and empathizing;

   • Being genuine by both agreeing and disagreeing.

3. Asking the partners to trade books for this activity provides the participants with permanent records for their comments.

4. It is important that the participants have the opportunity to comment on their experiences in the total group at the end of the interviews. This practice provides the participants with permanent records of their comments.

RELAXATION

All of the activities described in this chapter plus a short break can be completed in approximately three hours. This time schedule allows thirty minutes for a concluding relaxation experience. Use the instructions for progressive relaxation and meditation in the workbook (pp. 56 and 57, respectively) to create a twenty-minute experience for the participants. Be comfortable and familiar with these techniques before asking a group to try them.

Give the group a chance to share experiences and raise questions for a few minutes before closing for the day. Mention that although the workbook presents only three letting-go techniques (relaxation, meditation, and self-healing), the participants may wish to research and try several others, such as biofeedback. Suggest also that many good tapes of relaxation instructions are available, or the participants may want to create their own tapes from the workbook instructions for progressive relaxation.

REFERENCES

Mackenzie, R. A. The time trap. New York: AMACOM, 1972.
Webber, R. A. Time and management. New York: Van Nostrand Reinhold, 1972.

CHAPTER 6

THIRD SESSION

The third session begins with the presentation of the self-awareness activity, the Life-Style Preference Evaluation (workbook, p. 32), and the subsequent discussion of the participants' life-style orientations. Most of the time remaining after the completion of this activity is devoted to a diagnosis of the participants' support networks and action planning for improving these networks. The half-day session closes with a brief look at the prework data on the Episodic, Work-Related Stress Evaluation (workbook, p. 15) and the Chronic, Work-Related Stress Evaluation (workbook, p. 19); the presentation of these data sets the stage for the final session.

LIFE-STYLE PREFERENCES

Goals   To increase the participants' awareness of their individual orientations toward themselves, their peers, and authority.

To promote an understanding of the ways in which these orientations contribute to the experience of stress.

Format   Individual and total-group work.

Duration One hour.

Materials Life-Style Preference Evaluation (workbook, p. 32) and pencils.

Setting   Room large enough for the total group and with writing surfaces for the participants.

Process   1. Ask the participants to determine the extent of personal applicability of the twenty-four statements in the Life-

Style Preference Evaluation; do not have them total their responses according to category (personalistic, sociocentric, and formalistic).

2. Using the workbook materials, explain and discuss the three response categories.

3. Ask the participants to predict whether their scores will be high, medium, or low in each of the three categories.

4. Have the participants total their responses according to category and compare their scores with the statistics listed in the workbook in Table 5 (p. 35) and Table 6 (p. 36).

5. Lead a total-group discussion on the implications of the activity results.

Remarks   1. The point of using the Life-Style Preference Evaluation is to provide the participants with a degree of self-awareness to be integrated with other workshop learnings when final planning for improved stress management is undertaken at the end of the workshop.

Although many other ways exist to help participants become more self-aware, the Life-Style Preference Evaluation is particularly appropriate because it coordinates well with the organizational content of the workshop. Also, unlike some other methods of fostering self-awareness, it does not require that the participants take any significant interpersonal risks.

2. If the participants comprise an ongoing work group, have them share their scores and spend some time looking for ways to solve their common problems. Also have them determine which of the three orientations are rewarded in their working environment and which are not. In this discussion explore the ways in which the participants and the organization might reduce stress in the work environment.

SUPPORT-NETWORK REVIEW

Goals   To help the participants develop broad definitions of their support needs.

To increase the participants' awareness of their present needs for support and their satisfaction with existing supportive relationships.

To enable the participants to identify gaps in their individual support networks.

Format   Individual and total-group work.

Duration   Thirty minutes.

Materials   Support-Network Review (workbook, p. 62) and pencils.

Setting   Room large enough for the total group and with writing surfaces for the participants.

Process   1. Lecture and/or lead a discussion on the importance of an effective support network for maintaining health and perspective and for solving problems during stressful periods.

2. Ask the participants to complete the Support-Network Review.

3. Invite the participants to share their individual insights with the total group.

4. In preparation for the Support-Network Improvement Plan,[6] ask the participants to select up to six people with whom they would like improved support relationships and/or with whom they would like to establish new support relationships.

Remarks   1. Emphasize that *support* is defined broadly and not just as an individual's close friends.

2. During the total-group sharing of reactions, many participants will point out their discovery that they rely on too few people to satisfy too many support roles. Most

---

[6]The identification of the six people with whom each participant desires better or new relationships provides a bridge to the next topic, Support-Network Improvement. If this topic is to be omitted from the workshop design, either do not have the participants identify these six or simply have them do some thinking about possible advantageous changes in the identified relationships.

of the participants will be able to voice some dissatisfaction with their support networks as they have assessed them.

SUPPORT-NETWORK IMPROVEMENT

Goals   To help the participants analyze their present relationships with up to six other people.

To assist the participants in assessing their individual roles in creating or altering their support networks.

To identify specific steps for improving or establishing key support relationships.

Format   Individual work, work with partners, and total-group work.

Duration   One hour.

Materials   Support-Network Improvement Plan (workbook, p. 65) and pencils.

Setting   Room with writing surfaces for the participants and large enough to allow partners to work together without intrusion from other pairs.

Process   1. Ask the participants to complete the Support-Network Improvement Plan.

2. Have the partners consult each other regarding their proposed first action steps.

3. Spend some time sharing experiences in the total group.

Remarks   1. Emphasize the importance of identifying at least one action step for improving or establishing each relationship.

2. Point out to the participants that unless the other person in each identified relationship is also attending the workshop and has reciprocated the selection, the chances are slight that this person is making any current plans to alter the relationship. Thus, it is up to the

participants themselves to initiate any changes they desire in their selected relationships.

3. Encourage the partners to build on the rapport they have established in the previous activities and see how helpful they can be to each other in providing reality checks, suggesting different alternatives, and so on.

ORGANIZATIONAL STRESSORS

Goals

To introduce participants to possibilities for reducing unnecessary stress in an organization.

To review the participants' scores on the Episodic, Work-Related Stress Evaluation and the Chronic, Work-Related Stress Evaluation and to investigate a rank ordering of the items selected by the participants as the most stressful.

Format

Total-group work.

Duration

Thirty minutes.

Materials

Handouts listing the participants' greatest sources of episodic and chronic, work-related stress (derived from the completed prework evaluations on workbook pages 15 and 19, respectively).

Setting

Room large enough for the total group.

Process

1. Present again the participants' scores on the Episodic and Chronic, Work-Related Stress Evaluations in rank order from highest to lowest score for each type of evaluation.

2. Invite participant responses and questions.

3. For each type of evaluation, present and discuss a priority table of the greatest sources of stress. (At the end of each evaluation, the participants were asked to identify the three events or situations that they personally experienced as being the most stressful and to rank them in order of stressfulness from 1 to 3. Before the workshop convenes, use the participants' prework results to construct a priority table for each evaluation

type: Assign three points to the events or situations identified as most stressful, two points to those identified as second most stressful, and one point to those identified as third most stressful. A sample is provided in Table 1.)

4. Lead a discussion on those sources of stress that have relatively large priority totals. Solicit ideas for eliminating or coping with these high-priority stressors.

Table 1. Sample Priority Table of Greatest Sources of Episodic, Work-Related Stress

Item[a]	Rank	Event	Assigned Priority Points	Priority Total
1	3	Being transferred against my will to a new position or assignment	3,2,2	7
2	2	Being shelved (moved to a less important job)	1,2,3,2,1	9
3	8	Experiencing a decrease in status (either actual or in relation to my peers)	0	0
4	4	Being disciplined or seriously reprimanded by my supervisor	3,1,1,1	6
5	7	Having my request to transfer to a new, more satisfying job rejected	2	2
6	5	Sustaining a sudden, significant change in the nature of my work	1,3	4
7	6	Learning of the cancellation of a project I was involved with and considered important	1,2	3
8	1	Encountering major or frequent changes in instructions, policies, or procedures	3,3,3,2,1,3,2[b]	17
.	.	.	.	.
.	.	.	.	.
.	.	.	.	.

[a]Order assigned on Episodic, Work-Related Stress Evaluation

[b]If the participants are all from the same organization, the assigned priority points probably will cluster very clearly around specific stressors. Even if the participants are all strangers from different organizations, it is likely that the points will cluster somewhat. Identify the cluster patterns, and invite discussion of ways to eliminate or cope with the most widely selected stressors.

Remarks   1. Remind the participants that it is the *novelty impact* of the episodic stressors that causes most of their associated stress and that most chronic stressors are rooted in the social norms of the organization.

2. Suggest that the principal ways to avoid or remove stressors of these two types are to improve information flow, thereby reducing the element of novelty or surprise in necessary changes, and to alter stressor norms by means of developing commitments to change among the members of face-to-face work groups.

3. Discussion of the high-priority stressors may identify additional stressors not listed on the evaluations.

CHAPTER 7

FOURTH SESSION

The final half-day session focuses on organizational stress for the first one and a half hours, beginning with the completion and discussion of the Job-Suitability Analysis (workbook, p. 74), which allows the participants to assess their suitability for their work environments. Then subgroups are formed, each concentrating on a different group of common organizational stressors, developing a recommended plan of action for their alleviation, and presenting the proposed plan to the total group.

The rest of the session is devoted to the completion of the Workbook Review and Personal Action Plan (workbook, p. 91), an evaluation of the workshop, and a final relaxation experience.

JOB SUITABILITY

Goal   To increase the participants' awareness of their suitability for their jobs.

Format   Individual and total-group work.

Duration   Thirty minutes.

Materials   Job-Suitability Analysis (workbook, p. 74), pencils, newsprint flip charts, and felt-tipped markers.

Setting   Room large enough for the total group and with writing surfaces for the participants.

Process   1. Ask the participants to complete the Job-Suitability Analysis.

2. By a show of hands, tally the number of participants with discrepancies of 3, 4, and 5 or greater for any of the ten dimensions of the analysis.

3. Lecture and/or lead a discussion on the results and possible solutions to the problems presented. (Refer to the workbook text following the Job-Suitability Analysis.)

Remarks

1. The scoring system for the Job-Suitability Analysis will be unusual to most of the participants. Be sure to provide detailed instructions on scoring, and walk around the room offering individual assistance.

2. If the workshop participants comprise an ongoing work group, have them hand in their scores without identity on the papers. The scores probably will cluster; the clusters of large discrepancies (3, 4, and 5 or greater) will provide further focus on the areas in which stress should be reduced. Clustering is particularly apt to appear in the areas of relationships (with supervisors, peers, and subordinates).

3. This activity was derived from the ongoing work of the University of Michigan's Institute for Social Research at NASA's Goddard Center. For a good account of this work, refer to French and Caplan (1972).

ORGANIZATIONAL-IMPROVEMENT PROPOSALS

Goals

To confront the participants with the real nature of organizational stressors.

To help the participants develop realistic action proposals for dealing with these stressors.

Format

Work in groups of four to six (partners together) and total-group work.

Duration

One hour.

Materials

Paper, pencils, newsprint flip charts, and felt-tipped markers.

Setting   Room with writing surfaces for the participants and large enough to allow the entire group to meet in small subgroups.

Process   1. Instruct the participants to form groups of four to six members each, staying with their partners. Ask each group to spend twenty minutes developing a set of recommendations for dealing with organizational stressors.

2. Have each group briefly report its recommendations to the larger group, and solicit reactions. Allow twenty minutes for the entire process.

3. Lead a total-group discussion on organizational stressors and organizational change.

Remarks   1. It is helpful to present Figure 1 in this manual (p. 16) to the participants, assigning one or more of the small groups to work with each of the three types of stress response (removal or avoidance, immediate response, and long-term protection).

2. Because this experience emphasizes the difficulty of finding ways to implement organizational changes, the participants are likely to exhibit fatigue and frustration at this point. Thus, it may be necessary to help the total group respond to the various small-group proposals by suggesting various follow-up methods.

PERSONAL PLANNING

Goals   To help the participants review the workshop material and develop a clear view of their individual needs for improved stress management.

To help the participants identify the first steps to take in the improvement process.

Format   Individual work, work with partners, and total-group work.

Duration   One hour.

Materials   Workbook Review and Personal Action Plan (workbook, p. 91) and pencils.

Setting   Room with writing surfaces for the participants and large enough to allow the partners to work together without intrusion from other pairs.

Process   1. Ask the participants to complete the Workbook Review and Personal Action Plan. Allow twenty-five minutes for this activity.

2. Have the partners spend twenty-five minutes consulting each other regarding their needs for improved stress management.

3. Meet with the total group for final questions and observations.

EVALUATION

To receive feedback on the progress of the workshop, ask the participants to complete the Workshop Evaluation at the end of this chapter.

RELAXATION

For a closing experience, repeat the relaxation activity conducted at the close of the second half-day segment; or, if the participants have been unusually open to both relaxation and meditation, lead them through the self-healing experience (workbook, p. 58). As emphasized previously, be thoroughly familiar and comfortable with these techniques before using them with the participants.

DESIGN VARIATION

For various reasons it might be preferable to schedule the organizational segment as the second session and the self-management segment last. Either sequence works equally well, and the various segments are easily rearranged.

REFERENCE

French, J.R.P., Jr., & Caplan, R.D. Organizational stress and individual strain. In A. Marrow (Ed.), *The failure of success.* New York: AMACOM, 1972.

WORKSHOP EVALUATION

Name (optional) _____

Title in organization _____

I. Indicate how successful you felt the workshop to be in each of the following dimensions by circling the number of the response that best applies.

1. The organization of the
   workshop was 1 2 3 4 5 6 7 8 9 10
                                Poor   Excellent

2. Assess the achievement of
   the following objectives:

          OBJECTIVE   LEVEL OF ACHIEVEMENT

   a. To help me understand my
      physiological and
      psychological reactions to
      stress 1 2 3 4 5 6 7 8 9 10
                                    Not at All   Clearly
                                    Achieved   Achieved

   b. To help me diagnose my
      personal and organizational
      sources of stress 1 2 3 4 5 6 7 8 9 10
                                     Not at All   Clearly
                                     Achieved   Achieved

   c. To teach several practical
      approaches to stress
      management from both
      the individual and
      organizational perspectives ...1 2 3 4 5 6 7 8 9 10
                                      Not at All   Clearly
                                      Achieved   Achieved

| OBJECTIVE | LEVEL OF ACHIEVEMENT |

d. To help me develop a
   personal strategy for
   coping with and managing
   stressful events and
   situations 1 2 3 4 5 6 7 8 9 10
                              Not at All   Clearly
                              Achieved   Achieved

3. The work of the trainer(s) was . . 1 2 3 4 5 6 7 8 9 10
                                      Poor   Excellent

4. The scope (coverage) was 1 2 3 4 5 6 7 8 9 10
                                  Inadequate   Very
                                                         Adequate

5. The overall quality of the
   workshop was 1 2 3 4 5 6 7 8 9 10
                              Poor   Excellent

II. Answer the following questions.

1. What were the strongest features of the workshop? _____

   _____

   _____

2. What were the weakest features?_____

   _____

   _____

3. What *additional* topics would have enhanced the workshop
   curriculum?_____

   _____

   _____

4. On which topics should more time have been spent?_____

   _____

   _____

5. Was the total workshop duration adequate, or should it have
   been longer or shorter?_____

   _____

   _____

III. Write any other comments in the space below.